T0303780

TRANSITION ON THE WESTERN RAILWAYS

TIM SQUIRES

AMBERLEY

Front cover (top): A First GWR HST led by power car No. 43186 arrives at Bristol Parkway with 1L79, the 09.00 Penzance to London Paddington service, on 10 October 2018. It was taking this unusual route due to a line closure at Newbury.

Front cover (bottom): First GWR Class 802 Hitachi IET No. 802016 is seen approaching Exeter St Thomas with 1C79, the 11.01 London Paddington to Penzance service, on 6 October 2019.

Rear cover: GWR Class 143 Pacer No. 143617 is pictured basking in the sunshine at Exeter depot with a Class 153 for company on 5 May 2018.

First published 2021

Amberley Publishing
The Hill, Stroud
Gloucestershire, GL5 4EP

www.amberley-books.com

Copyright © Tim Squires, 2021

The right of Tim Squires to be identified as the Author of this work has been asserted in accordance with the Copyrights, Designs and Patents Act 1988.

ISBN 978 1 3981 0275 0 (print)
ISBN 978 1 3981 0276 7 (ebook)

All rights reserved. No part of this book may be reprinted or reproduced or utilised in any form or by any electronic, mechanical or other means, now known or hereafter invented, including photocopying and recording, or in any information storage or retrieval system, without the permission in writing from the Publishers.

British Library Cataloguing in Publication Data.
A catalogue record for this book is available from the British Library.

Typesetting by SJmagic DESIGN SERVICES, India.
Printed in Great Britain.

Introduction

Sometimes, it's only by looking back through photographs that we realise how much things have changed in a reasonably short space of time, and that is most definitely the case with the past five years on the former BR Western Region. This book consists of a collection of pictures taken between 2015 and the start of 2020 – a time of development in the area, such as the region's dominant train operating company, First Great Western, embracing the past and undergoing a major rebranding exercise. It became GWR (Great Western Railway) in the autumn of 2015, although the often troubled FGW brand is still clearly evident to this day, both at stations and on rolling stock.

Meanwhile, the Great Western Main Line electrification project was scaled back to the core route from London to Cardiff, as well as the fairly short stretch between Reading and Newbury. Sections including Didcot to Oxford and Cardiff to Swansea were 'paused' by Network Rail. These could potentially be reviewed at some point in the future, although this is by no means guaranteed.

Perhaps the most notable change for enthusiasts, however, has been the replacement of the venerable InterCity 125/HST fleet, with their successors being the Class 800 and 802 InterCity Express Train (IET) fleet, built by Japanese company Hitachi as part of their AT300 series of trains. These sets have 'bi-mode' capability and can therefore operate on both AC electric or diesel power – plans for units to solely run on electric were dropped after the changes to the electrification scheme. The Class 800s were procured by the Department for Transport, but to allow complete replacement of HSTs on front-line duties in the west of England, more trains were required. First have therefore leased another thirty-six sets, designated as Class 802, which are closely related to the 800s.

However, this isn't quite the end for HSTs in the region, as GWR has opted to retain some in short four-coach formations for regional services. These refurbished sets have been reclassified as Class 255 and given the designation 'Castle Class' by GWR, with each power car carrying the name of a local castle. CrossCountry's small fleet of HSTs also remain in daily service from the North to the South West.

Major changes have also been seen in GWR's fleet of local and regional services, with a large-scale cascade of units kick-started by the introduction of new Class 378 electric units for Thames Valley local services, which has allowed most 'Network Turbo' units to be transferred to Bristol, with the Class 158s then heading to Devon and Cornwall. One of the final pieces of the jigsaw is the proposed Class 769 Flex – this project involves diesel engines being fitted to dual-voltage Class 319 EMUs by Brush Traction. The units will then be used on a variety of services in the Thames Valley area, enabling more Turbos to be moved to Bristol. Unfortunately the plan has been delayed due to issues in the 769 conversion process.

Additional changes have been due to accessibility legislation for passengers with restricted mobility, requiring extensive modification to most older trains and the withdrawal of others. GWR's Class 153 fleet has been moved on to Transport for Wales, who have undertaken the work to allow further service, while the Class 143 Pacers were withdrawn from service in December 2020 with most being scrapped. Improvements have also been made to many stations to allow better access.

December 2019 saw the biggest timetable change on the Great Western since 1976, with around 75 per cent of services being revised. The main purpose was to take advantage of the IET's superior performance, but there have also been improvements to services throughout the majority of the network. The new timetable was given widespread publicity to make passengers aware of the changes, and thankfully it had a trouble-free introduction compared to the well-documented issues on the Thameslink network.

My earliest railway memories are being taken to Exeter St Davids station in the summer of 2001 at around five years old. There were lots of Valenta-powered HSTs to be seen, along with the end of Class 47-hauled services and considerably more freight workings than you would find today. A few years later and my early enthusiasm had almost been forgotten in favour of other interests, until we reach 2011, when I purchased a cheap compact digital camera and very quickly found that I enjoyed taking pictures on my travels, especially of the trains that I encountered!

That cheap compact only lasted around a year before giving up on life, but it had got me hooked on railway photography, and so after a couple of camera upgrades I settled on Nikon DSLRs. Most of the images in this book are taken with either a D5200 or the D7200 that replaced it in 2016. In terms of lenses, I have a few to choose from, but I usually use a Nikkor 35 mm prime lens, which I favour for both its low weight and high image quality.

This book is not intended to be a comprehensive account of every change that has taken place, but acts as a snapshot of an interesting time in the area's railway history. I particularly enjoy being out with a camera on the famous stretch of line between Exeter and Newton Abbot, which I feel has a unique character, and I am fortunate to live within an hour of this location. I have tried to select a wide variety of images, particularly focusing on the evolution of the HST fleet, but not forgetting the local units, freight services, and a few interesting developments on the heritage railways in the area.

FGW Class 153 No. 153329 is seen dwarfed by the platform used to help raise the part of the Dawlish Sea Wall that was damaged by a winter storm in February 2014, which led to a washout that closed the line for months. The 153 is operating 2T14, the 12.49 Exeter St Davids to Paignton service, on 28 January 2015.

DB Schenker Class 66 No. 66101 stands at Westbury with 6P62, the 19:25 Westbury Up T.C. to West Ruislip engineers working, on 25 February 2015. Although the red livery was first introduced in 2009, locomotives can still be found in the livery of EWS, who were taken over by DB, although they have subsequently rebranded again as DB Cargo UK.

A view of FGW Class 150/1 Sprinter No. 150124 arriving at St Austell with 2P86, the 11.41 Penzance to Plymouth service, on 18 February 2015. The rough-looking signal box dates from 1905, however it was closed in March 1980, with control passing to Par. Its continued survival is down to its listed structure status.

First Great Western HSTs from the West Country were diverted to London Waterloo over Easter 2015 due to engineering work at Reading. Here, Class 43 No. 43071 stands at Waterloo shortly after arriving with 1O36, the 11.07 arrival from Exeter St Davids, on Easter Sunday, 5 April 2015.

In early 2015 FGW introduced two 'Building a Greater West' branded HST power cars. Here the seaside-themed No. 43146 is seen shortly after leaving Tiverton Parkway with 1C87, the 15.57 London Paddington to Plymouth service, on 3 May 2015.

A regular sight for many years was First Great Western using a South West Trains Class 158, although this arrangement has now ceased. Here No. 158883 stands at Gloucester with 2G89, the 18.14 Swindon to Cheltenham Spa service, on 6 June 2015. The spire of St Peter's Church can be seen on the left of the image.

Direct Rail Services Class 57/3 No. 57303 *Pride of Carlisle* is seen at Plymouth while on hire to First Great Western, powering 2P70, the 12.31 arrival from Par, on 20 June 2015 – the fifth consecutive week this locomotive had worked FGW's summer Saturday loco-hauled service that operated between 2014 and 2018.

An FGW HST set led by Class 43 No. 43088 is seen passing Cockwood Foot Crossing with 1A92, the slightly delayed 15.06 Newquay to London Paddington service, on Wednesday 12 August 2015.

FGW Class 43 No. 43193 is standing at Carmarthen while operating 1B15, the 08.45 London Paddington to Pembroke Dock service, on 22 August 2015. This summer Saturday-only route requires two reversals – both here and earlier in the journey at Swansea.

A classic scene from London Paddington as a line-up of HST power cars await their next workings on 17 September 2015. The green power car nearest the camera is No. 43187, which had been part of the launch event for the GWR brand earlier that week.

Class 43 power car No. 43188 is seen at Newton Abbot leading the original GWR green liveried HST set away from the now mothballed Heathfield Branch while operating 1Z70, the 16.42 Heathfield to London Paddington leg of the Branch Line Society's 'First Devon & Exeter Explorer' railtour, on 10 October 2015.

Due to Crossrail related engineering works, GWR HSTs were diverted away from London Paddington in the period after Christmas 2015, with Swansea services using London Marylebone after reversing at Banbury. Here, No. 43148 is at Marylebone with 1Z29, the 17.32 to Swansea, on 27 December 2015. This was one of three power cars to wear 'Bristol 2015' branding, in connection with the city's then European Green Capital status.

An image from the early part of the transition phase in the GWR HST fleet as Class 43 No. 43168 leads an otherwise green-liveried set past Exminster Marshes on 1C83, the 13.05 London Paddington to Plymouth service, on 10 February 2016.

Network Rail Class 31 No. 31285 suffered a failure while operating a test train in Devon and became a long-term resident of the sidings in Exeter's Riverside Yard, finally being removed on 9 March 2016 after being sold to Harry Needle Railway Company. It was subsequently acquired by the Weardale Railway. The locomotive is pictured on 6 March 2016.

FGW Class 150/2 No. 150219 was released from an overhaul in April 2015 with the addition of a large accessible toilet and an automated PA system, plus extra bicycle space. The downside of this refurbishment was a considerable loss of seating. It has been carried out on all FGW/ GWR Class 150/2s to make them compliant with accessibility regulations that took effect on 1 January 2020.

Due to gauging issues, the UK Railtours 'Tre, Pol and Pen' tour on 6 March 2016 was unable to visit the Parkandillack line in Cornwall as planned, so after Fowey Docks the train also ran to Plymouth Friary and Meldon Quarry, with traction being two DB Cargo Class 66s. Here, No. 66177 (fitted with experimental white cab roofs to keep internal temperatures down) is approaching the buffer stops of the rarely used Plymouth Friary line. It is running as 1Z52 from London Euston.

A GWR HST led by No. 43094 is seen passing Oath – located on the Somerset Levels between Castle Cary and Taunton – while operating 1C85, the 14.00 London Paddington to Penzance service, on 2 April 2016.

At the rear of 1C86, the 15.00 Paddington-Penzance service on 2 April 2016, we find the other 'Building a Greater West' branded Class 43, No. 43144, which carried countryside-style images. The power cars carried these liveries long into the GWR era, with No. 43144 the longer lasting of the pair.

A pair of GWR Class 143s, No. 143618 with No. 143603 in tow, are seen at Yeoford while operating 2F35, the 13.43 Barnstaple to Exmouth service, on 9 April 2016. The somewhat disused-looking track to the left is actually the Okehampton branch line, usually only used on summer Sundays.

Freightliner Class 47/8 No. 47830 *Beeching's Legacy* was used by Rail Operations Group for a GWR stock move consisting of refurbished HST trailer vehicles on 9 April 2016. It is seen here about to pass Tiverton Parkway, running around three hours early, as 5V56 – the 06.00 Kilmarnock Barclay to Plymouth Laira depot.

On 17 April 2016 the UK Railtours 'Tarka Tourer' charter ran from London Paddington to Barnstaple using a First GWR HST, becoming the first 125 set to visit the branch since 1985. Here, No. 43165 *Prince Michael of Kent* has just arrived at Barnstaple with the empty stock move ahead of the return working.

In this view, the return leg of the 'Tarka Tourer' is seen approaching Umberleigh level crossing operating as 1Z18, the 16.30 Barnstaple to London Paddington, with No. 43128 leading and No. 43165 now on the rear.

A slow (1/80 sec.) shutter-speed captures the essence of speed as a GWR HST set with No. 43009 leading passes Stoke Canon level crossing, around 4 miles north of Exeter, while operating the 1A95 16.07 Plymouth to Paddington service on 17 April 2016.

The sign says it all as GWR Class 153 No. 153377 is seen at Liskeard bound for Looe on 2L79, the 11.11 service on 21 April 2016. Despite not requiring the capacity of a two carriage train, this branch line is now operated with Class 150/2s after the departure of the 153 fleet.

Long Rock depot-based Class 08 shunters used to be a common sight at Penzance stations in connection with the empty stock movements for the overnight sleeper service, but these are now carried out with the Class 57 piloting the train in and out. Here No. 08410 stands at Penzance after earlier bringing in the ECS for the London-bound service on 21 April 2016.

A view of the HST line-up exhibited at the Bristol St Philip's Marsh depot open day held in aid of the Springboard Opportunity Group charity on bank holiday Monday, 2 May 2016.
From left to right: No. 43172 *Harry Patch*; No. 43423 *Valenta 1972–2010*; No. 43013; No. 43300 *Craigentinny*; 43048 *T.C.B Miller MBE*; and No. 43187.

Another highlight of the open day was the unveiling of GWR Class 43 No. 43002 in the original BR InterCity 125 livery, along with a ceremony to name it *Sir Kenneth Grange* in honour of the designer of the production Class 43 cab. This power car is now part of the National Railway Museum's collection.

GWR Class 150/2 No. 150266 is seen at Avonmouth while operating 2K36, the 17.16 Bristol Temple Meads to Severn Beach service, on bank holiday Monday 2 May 2016. This unit is wearing the 'local lines' version of FGW livery, in which the lines on the bodyside were made up of the names of places of interest along the routes served by the trains.

Due to increased cycle use of the Exe Estuary Trail, a new footbridge was constructed at Powderham in 2014 to replace a foot crossing – it also provides a useful photographic vantage point. In this view, a GWR HST led by Class 43 No. 43063 is leading 1C84, the 14.07 London Paddington to Penzance service, past the footbridge on 18 May 2016.

A GWR HST led by Class 43 No. 43031 is seen after leaving Dawlish station while operating 2Z50, the 17.54 Exeter St Davids to Newton Abbot, on 28 May 2016. This was an extra service provided due to the Radio 1 Big Weekend being held at Powderham Castle, near Starcross.

The signal box at Truro is a Great Western Railway Type 7A design, built in 1899, and still in use to this day, with a large amount of Cornwall's signalling system remaining of the mechanical variety. A plan to close the manual boxes and move control to Exeter PSB has been put on hold, although a signalling improvement project has increased capacity.

GWR Class 43 HST power car No. 43172 was given this special livery and named *Harry Patch – The Last Survivor of the Trenches* in November 2015 to mark the centenary of the First World War. It is viewed here at Weston-super-Mare before trailing 1A29, the 18.08 service to London Paddington, on 22 June 2016.

GWR Class 43 No. 43027 carried this branding to commemorate Queen Elizabeth II's 90th birthday, as seen in this view of the power car pulling away from Exeter St Davids while operating 1A91, the 16.02 Plymouth to London Paddington service, on 29 June 2016.

Back-to-back power car moves for testing purposes were a common sight in South Devon when First were operating full-length HST formations. Here Nos 43180 and 43009 are passing Kingskerswell running as 0Z77, the 14.40 Laira to Laira via Newton Abbot, on 10 July 2016.

The unusually named 'The Herd of Wildebeest' charter ran on 16 July 2016, promoted by UK Railtours and powered by a total of four GBRf Class 73s. The tour was planned to start at London Waterloo, but had to be started from Basingstoke, with passengers being forwarded on a normal service. Unfortunately with the Class 73/1s leading from Exeter to Paignton, No. 73128 overheated near Newton Abbot, and the train arrived in Paignton just under an hour late. In this view, the train arrives at Paignton running as 1Z73, the 09.17 from Basingstoke.

GWR Class 153 No. 153370 is leading No. 153369 into Penryn while operating 2F85, the 16.20 Truro to Falmouth Docks service, on 28 September 2016. In the background No. 150233 is waiting for the signal to clear to allow it to proceed towards Truro.

Virgin Trains branded Hitachi Class 800 IET No. 800101 became the first of the new trains to run south of Bristol and into Devon as it operated a test run on 3 October 2016. It is seen waiting for a path forward from Exeter St Davids, running as 5X30, the 21.10 Stoke Gifford to Plymouth. This unit finally entered passenger service in spring 2020.

The Severn Tunnel was closed for six weeks in autumn 2016 for electrification work, which meant GWR HST services to and from South Wales had to run via Gloucester. Here No. 43179 *Pride of Laira* is running on the diversionary route at Chepstow while leading 1L68, the 13.28 Swansea to London Paddington service, on 12 October 2016.

DB Cargo Class 60 No. 60019 *Port of Grimsby & Immingham* is seen applying power away from a signal check at Gloucester station while operating 6B33, the 13.00 Theale Murco to Robeston petroleum tanks working, on 12 October 2016. Class 60s are still the regular traction for these trains.

The connection from the main line to the West Somerset Railway at Norton Fitzwarren has seen plenty of charter trains in recent years – LMS Princess Royal Class No. 6201 *Princess Elizabeth* has just used it while operating the outward leg of a Railway Touring Company excursion from London Paddington to Minehead on 22 October 2016.

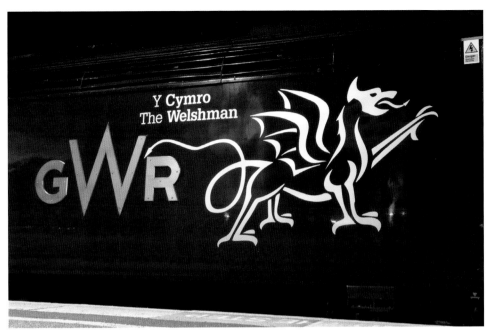

To mark the reopening of the Severn Tunnel after the lengthy closure, GWR marked the occasion by giving HST power cars Nos 43187 and 43188 bilingual branding of *Y Cymro/The Welshman*, which also became one of GWR's named services, given to the 07.28 Swansea to Paddington service.

The CrossCountry service from Devon to Manchester was subject to a timetable consultation that proposed cutting back the service south of Exeter in December 2017 – but this did not come to pass. In this view Class 220 Voyager No. 220016 is approaching its station stop at Dawlish with 1M41, the 10.06 Paignton to Manchester Piccadilly service, on 7 January 2017.

GWR Class 43s Nos 43156 and 43035 are seen stabled at Long Rock depot, Penzance, on the evening of 15 January 2017. This image is taken from a public road adjacent to the depot – there are also excellent views from the South West Coast Path, which runs alongside it.

This GWR HST, led by No. 43023 *Squadron Leader Harold Starr*, has just arrived at London Paddington after operating 1P16, the 07.06 from Didcot Parkway, on 24 January 2017. The magnificent train shed dates from 1854 when the station opened, and has been extensively (and rather expensively!) renovated.

Early in 2015, Class 153 No. 153325 was given this one-off livery promoting the Citizens' Rail international railway development project. The livery continued to be carried for around four years after the project ended, when the unit was transferred to Transport for Wales. Here it can be seen stabled at Exeter depot on 1 March 2017.

The North American-built Class 66 fleet are undoubtedly the backbone of freight services in this country, despite being unpopular with some enthusiasts due to their sheer numbers. In this view, DB Cargo No. 66080 is stabled at Didcot Parkway on 11 March 2017. Note the DB stickers applied to the old EWS livery.

The Turbo units were the backbone of local services in the Thames Valley prior to the arrival of the Class 387s. Here Class 165 No. 165127 is seen leading Class 166 No. 166202 as they arrive at Reading with 1P47, the 12.06 Worcester Foregate Street to London Paddington GWR service, on 11 March 2017.

Reading station is virtually unrecognisable from its previous appearance before the major remodelling project that took place between 2009 and 2015. Here, a GWR HST led by No. 43041 *Meningitis Trust – Support For Life* pauses at the station while operating 1A25, the 16.30 Bristol Temple Meads to London Paddington service, on 11 March 2017.

GWR's Class 387 Electrostars first entered service on 5 September 2016. No. 387140 is captured passing Royal Oak while operating 2S28, the 12.15 London Paddington to Hayes & Harlington service, on 29 March 2017. The rather substantial looking bridge above the train carries an approach road to the A40 Westway.

The Class 180 Adelante units have a chequered history on the Great Western franchise, with the entire fleet handed back by 2009 due to poor reliability, although five did subsequently return in 2012, remaining in service until 2017, when they transferred to Grand Central. No. 180106 is seen passing the London Underground station at Royal Oak with 1P40, the 09.54 Great Malvern to London Paddington service, on 29 March 2017.

The two prototype Class 150 DMUs were in service with GWR from 2012 until 2020, after being transferred from London Midland. In this view, No. 150002 is seen passing Stapleton Road while operating 2E36, the late-running 17.41 Bristol Temple Meads to Gloucester service, on 12 April 2017.

The glint of a stunning spring sunset is viewed along the bodyside of a CrossCountry HST set trailed by power car No. 43357 at Bristol Parkway on 12 April 2017.

Wearing a special livery for the Springboard charity, GWR Class 158 No. 158798 stands at Bristol Temple Meads while operating 1F20, the 13.23 Portsmouth Harbour to Cardiff Central service, on 2 May 2017. This unit received a repaint into standard GWR colours in 2018.

Class 150s were the standard offering on the Severn Beach branch prior to the introduction of the Turbo units. Here No. 150233 is seen pausing at Clifton Down with 2K34, the slightly delayed 16.35 Bristol Temple Meads to Avonmouth service, on 2 May 2017.

A GWR HST led by No. 43136 is captured sweeping past Marlands, just east of the exit of Whiteball Tunnel on the Devon/Somerset border, while operating 1C81, the 11.57 London Paddington to Penzance service, on 7 May 2017.

No. 43002 *Sir Kenneth Grange* at the unusual location of Bishops Lydeard on the West Somerset Railway on 13 May 2017 after operating 1Z66, the 08.36 'Somerset Explorer' charity charter from London Paddington. The train was supposed to run through to Minehead, but operational issues prevented it, meaning WSR resident D1010 *Western Campaigner* was supplied to take passengers to the seaside resort and back.

Colas took over the contract to operate the Network Rail infrastructure monitoring trains in September 2015. In this view, No. 37099 *Merl Evans 1947–2016* is seen at Newquay just before midnight on 17 May 2017 while operating 3Q53, the 20.42 Penzance to Exeter Riverside ultrasonic test train. The working was around forty minutes late at this point after requiring attention due to a coolant leak.

CrossCountry's HST sets provide useful extra capacity on services to and from the South West. Here No. 43285 is seen leading an XC set on the climb towards the summit at Whiteball Tunnel, on the Devon/Somerset border. It is leading 1S53, the 12.25 Plymouth to Edinburgh service, on 21 May 2017.

A view of a GWR HST led by power car No. 43063 passing Plymtree Overbridge, Cullompton, while operating 1C85, the 13.57 London Paddington to Plymouth service, on 21 May 2017. The M5 motorway runs alongside the railway in this area.

GWR Class 158 Express Sprinter No. 158958 is seen at Portsmouth Harbour before operating 1F24, the 14.08 to Cardiff Central, on 11 June 2017. The station is built on a wooden pier over the harbour and is extensively used for connections to ferries bound for the Isle of Wight.

Newquay station is by some margin the busiest station on the Atlantic Coast Line, as well as being the terminus, usually seeing over ten times more passengers a year than the total figures of the intermediate stations put together. In this view, GWR Class 150/1 No. 150120 is operating 2N07, the 15.01 service to Par, on Wednesday 21 June 2017.

GWR Class 153 No. 153361 is seen with No. 153382 at Penmere on the Falmouth branch line with 2F87, the 17.27 Truro to Falmouth Docks, on 21 June 2017. These units were frequent performers on the line, which is now solely Class 150 operated.

The unusual sight of a Freightliner Class 66 on a railtour as No. 66525 passes Rewe, near Exeter, while powering 1Z45, the 16.07 Penzance to Worcester Shrub Hill return leg of Pathfinder Tours' Mazey Day Cornishman excursion, on 24 June 2017. The day had begun very differently with DRS Class 37s in charge – unfortunately No. 37059 failed shortly after departure from Worcester, and No. 37069 was rumoured to be suffering power issues, so the Class 66 was scrambled to assist after earlier working a container train.

Plymouth Laira depot-based GWR Class 08 shunter No. 08641 is viewed here shunting a rake of HST trailer vehicles along Laira Embankment in the evening sunshine on Saturday 8 July 2017.

The 'local lines' livery FGW Class 150/2 was once a ubiquitous sight across the South West. One of the last survivors was No. 150249, which is seen at a rather wet Taunton while operating 2M74, the 21.36 to Bristol Temple Meads, on 30 July 2017.

Colas Rail operated a cement flow from South Wales to Cornwall from November 2016 until November 2020, usually hauled by a Class 70 locomotive with occasional appearances from Class 66 motive power. No. 70806 is seen here passing Rewe (just north of Exeter) with 6C36, the 11.38 Moorswater to Aberthaw empty cement tanks, on 17 August 2017.

Colas have also become a regular sight on Network Rail engineers workings in the South West. Here Class 70 No. 70815 is viewed waiting in the Down Through line at Plymouth station with 6C22, the 18.31 Westbury to Truro working consisting of five Network Rail auto-ballasters, on 30 August 2017.

Due to a registration issue with rostered steam locomotive No. 46100 *Royal Scot*, West Coast Railway Company Class 57 No. 57314 (the former No. 47372) was used to power the 'Royal Duchy' charter on 3 September 2017. In this view the WCRC 57 is seen passing Totnes in torrential rain running as 1Z37, the 08.52 Bristol Temple Meads to Par.

On 3 September 2017 Railcare's 'RailVac' RAUK-3 is hard at work in an engineering blockade at Exeter St Davids, which closed both platforms and the lines to Exeter Central. The 'RailVac' works like a giant vacuum cleaner, drawing up contaminated ballast from between (and underneath) the rails.

The IETs were tested extensively before they finally entered revenue-earning service on 16 October 2017. Many of the test runs were operated by GBRf, as was the case in this view of No. 800006 slowing to a stop at Tiverton Parkway with 5X30, the 14.03 London Paddington to Tiverton Loop working, on 8 September 2017.

Direct Rail Services Class 37s No. 37605 and No. 37606 were used to test Network Rail's Taunton-based independent snowploughs (ADB965231 and ADB96520) on 20 September 2017. In this view, the unusual consist is passing Tiverton Parkway with the return leg of the trip, running as 7Z09, the 16.21 Fairwater Yard to Fairwater Yard via Exeter Riverside.

The GWR Turbo units have settled down on the Bristol area local services. Class 166 No. 166212 is seen arriving at Lawrence Hill with 2K36, the 17.13 Bristol Temple Meads to Severn Beach service, on 4 October 2017.

An unwelcome sight for passengers at Bristol Parkway as GWR Class 153 No. 153377 appears on its own working 9M98, the delayed 12.27 Southampton Central to Great Malvern, on 18 October 2017. After continuing to lose time the service was terminated early at Worcester Shrub Hill. This working normally ran as 2M98 but was given the Class 9 reporting number as 153s are out of gauge east of Southampton Central.

GWR Class 800 No. 800005 (coupled to No. 800006, out of sight at the rear) is seen at Cardiff Central operating 1B40, the 13.45 London Paddington to Swansea service, on a very grey Wednesday 18 October 2017, the third day in passenger service for the IETs. A London Paddington-bound HST trailed by No. 43029 can be seen on the right.

A view of the standard class interior of a GWR Class 802 IET. The seats have come in for criticism from some quarters for their firmness, although the legroom is much better than the Mark 3 HST coaches, and there are also considerably more tables provided.

The First Class interior in GWR's InterCity Express Trains looks relatively basic for a premium offering, especially in comparison with the design latterly used on the HSTs, but a Pullman dining service is still available, with every set having a full kitchen.

GWR's Castle HST sets only convey standard class accommodation, with no catering facilities and high-density layout, with few tables – giving these sets over three-hundred seats in total. This is the interior of a Trailer Standard vehicle with wheelchair facilities, which have all seating facing in the same direction.

The Railhead Treatment Train (RHTT) is an important weapon in the railway industry's fight against poor rail conditions in the autumn leaf-fall season. DB Cargo Class 66 No. 66024 is seen at Bristol Temple Meads operating 3S59, the 20.32 working from Barton Hill, on 18 October 2017. The Bristol area RHTT has more recently been operated by Colas Rail.

Plymouth Laira-based GWR Class 08 shunter No. 08644 *Laira Diesel Depot 50 Years* was a guest at the South Devon Railway's 2017 diesel gala. In this view, the Gronk has just left Staverton with autocoach No. 150735 on the 13.31 short trip to Buckfastleigh on 4 November.

Taken with a telephoto lens from 'Forty Steps' footbridge, a GWR HST led by power car No. 43015 leads 1C83, the 13.05 London Paddington to Plymouth, out of Taunton station on 29 November 2017. The flats built at Firepool Lock have drastically changed the backdrop, as seen here.

Into the first full year in service for the IETs. GWR Class 800 No. 800017 is seen standing at Bristol Temple Meads with 1A09, the 07.12 Taunton to London Paddington service, on 2 February 2018. No. 800014 was the rear set.

A GWR HST led by Class 43 power car No. 43018 is seen arriving at Worcester Foregate Street with 1W00, the 08.21 London Paddington to Hereford service, on 2 February 2018. Diagrams on the Cotswold Line route are now operated by IET units in a variety of formations.

GWR Class 387 Electrostar No. 387152 is viewed arriving at Slough with 2P53, the 14.48 Reading to London Paddington service, on 2 February 2018. The light beside the coupler provides illumination for a track-recording camera, and is fitted as standard on the 387s.

The Turbo units still rule the roost on the Thames branch lines. Class 165 No. 165132 stands at Marlow before operating 2B39, the 16.05 service back to Maidenhead, on 2 February 2018.

GWR Class 165 No. 165118 is seen here at the branch-line terminus of Henley-on-Thames before operating 2H49, the 17.05 service to Twyford, on 2 February 2018.

USA-built S160 Class No. 5197 was hired to the Paignton & Dartmouth Steam Railway from the Churnet Valley Railway, making for an unusual sight in Devon. In this view, the loco is seen leaving Kingswear with the 14.45 service to Paignton on 11 February 2018. Despite the bright sunshine it was a bitterly cold day with a sleet shower falling!

GWR Class 57/6 No. 57603 *Tintagel Castle* stands at Paddington on the morning of 17 February 2018 after leading 1A40, the 21.45 Night Riviera sleeper from Penzance. The Mark 3 coaches used on this service were given a major refurbishment during 2017/8, adding more capacity in the seated coaches, while the sleeping accommodation was modernised, with a wheelchair-accessible cabin fitted.

GWR Legends of the Great Western branded Class 43 HST power car No. 43093 *Old Oak Common HST Depot 1976–2018* is pictured at St Austell with 5Z46, the 15.02 Truro to Exeter St Davids 2+4 HST test run on 21 March 2018.

InterCity-liveried Class 43 No. 43185 *Great Western* is seen passing Dawlish Warren leading 1C86, the 15.03 London Paddington to Penzance GWR service, on 18 April 2018. At the time of writing, this power car was being used as a parts donor at Scotrail's Haymarket depot.

Arriva XC Class 221 Super Voyager No. 221144 is viewed at Paignton station after shunting from Platform 1 to operate 1M80, the 20.14 service to Birmingham New Street, on 2 May 2017. This unit was formed in 2016 from the driving cars of the original No. 221144 and two intermediate coaches from XC's other Class 221s.

A GWR HST led by Class 43 No. 43133 is seen arriving at Bodmin Parkway with 1A20, the 10.00 Penzance to London Paddington service, on Saturday 5 May 2018. The trackbed condition perhaps leaves a little to be desired for a station on the Cornish Main Line!

The stretch of line from Thingley Junction (near Chippenham) through Bath and on to Bristol had its planned electrification postponed indefinitely after the costs of the project soared. Here Freightliner Class 66/5 No. 66539 passes Chippenham station with 6X04, the 13.45 Kennet Bridge to Taunton engineers working, on 13 May 2018.

Class 43 No. 43040 *Bristol St Philips Marsh* is seen arriving at Tiverton Parkway with 1C87, the 15.22 London Paddington to Plymouth GWR service, on 3 June 2018. This station is around 7 miles by road from Tiverton town centre, but is well used by passengers from North Devon and even Cornwall due to its proximity to the M5 motorway.

The other surviving prototype Class 150, No. 150001, is seen passing Creech St Michael (near Taunton) with 2E81, the 18.30 Bristol Temple Meads to Exeter St Davids service, on 3 June 2018. Both units left GWR in April 2020 and were transferred to Northern.

GWR Class 150/1 No. 150126 is seen passing Plymtree Overbridge, Cullompton, with Class 153s Nos 153329 and 153372 in tow while operating 2C56, the 14.37 Penzance to Bristol Temple Meads service, on 10 June 2018. Two years later and all of these units had moved on to pastures new.

GWR's West of England to London services were diverted via Honiton and Yeovil for three days in June 2018 due to flood defence work at Cowley Bridge Junction (Exeter). Here, a green HST set led by blue power car No. 43086 is viewed approaching Exeter Central with 1C82, the 13.03 London Paddington to Penzance service, on 12 June.

In another image taken during the Cowley Bridge closure, a GWR HST led by Class 43 No. 43078 is arriving at Honiton while operating 1A88, the 12.04 Penzance to London Paddington service, on 13 June 2018. Due to the long single-line sections on the ex-Southern Region route, services are rather prone to delays during GWML diversions, as the diverted trains cause pressure on the timetable.

An unusual visitor to Devon, Hastings DEMU No. 1001 is seen waiting in Goodrington Sidings, Paignton before operating 1Z66, the 17.21 to Hastings return leg of the South Devon Coaster charter, on 16 June 2018.

GWR Class 57 No. 57605 *Totnes Castle* is running alongside the Exe Estuary at Starcross while operating 2C51, the 17.50 Exeter St Davids to Penzance service, on 23 June 2018. This locomotive was new as Class 47 No. 47206 before being fitted with a refurbished EMD engine by Brush Traction as part of the Class 57 conversion programme.

GWR Class 158 Express Sprinter No. 158763 is captured passing Exminster with 2P93, the 15.51 Exeter St Davids to Plymouth service, on 5 July 2018. This was the last Class 158 to wear the old FGW Dynamic Lines livery and, like the others, has now been repainted into GWR green colours.

A4 Pacific No. 60009 *Union of South Africa* operated the Torbay Express excursion on Sunday 15 July 2018, but due to lineside fire risks during an extremely hot and dry summer, diesel-powered assistance was provided in the form of DBC Class 66 No. 66106. Here, the unusual pairing are passing Kingskerswell (just south of Newton Abbot) running as 1Z28, the 16.50 Kingswear to Bristol Temple Meads.

The railway around Cowley Bridge Junction, Exeter, has in the past been extremely liable to flooding, but the drainage work carried out appears to have finally improved the matter, although the line was closed in February 2020 after a period of heavy rain. Here, Class 802 No. 802101 is passing the junction with 5Z22, the 11.03 London Paddington to Exeter St Davids working, on 24 July 2018.

The FGW/GWR summer Sunday service from Exeter to Okehampton has been operated with various DMUs over the years, with the most recent traction being the Class 150/2. In this view, we find No. 150232 standing at Okehampton station with 2E27, the 17.59 to St Davids, on 12 August 2018. Daily services on the line are expected to start in late 2021.

A GWR HST led by Class 43 No. 43087 *11 Explosive Ordnance Disposal Regiment – Royal Logistics Corps* is seen passing Dawlish with 1A87, the 12.00 Penzance to Paddington service, on 18 August 2018. This viewpoint has now changed after work was carried out to raise the edge of the sea wall to provide more resilience against the water.

Former Northern Class 150/2 No. 150207 was sent to GWR in exchange for the DMS vehicles from units Nos 150209 and 150212, and was operated for some time in the livery of its previous operator before being repainted, as viewed here at St James' Park (Exeter) after working 2J92, the 16.08 from Exeter St Davids, on 3 September 2018.

Off-lease and unbranded GWR HST power cars Nos 43177/43176, with TFD No. 41010 sandwiched in the middle, are pictured passing Tiverton Parkway with 5Z83, the 08.37 Laira depot to Bristol Temple Meads working, on 10 October 2018. The consist then continued to Ely for storage.

GWR Class 800 No. 800028 is seen arriving at Bristol Parkway with No. 800008 in tow while operating 1L55, the 11.29 Swansea to London Paddington service, on 10 October 2018. The electrification equipment had recently been installed when this image was taken and the first passenger train used it on New Year's Eve 2018.

Platform 1 at Bristol Parkway was opened in April 2018, increasing the capacity at this busy station. GWR Class 165 No. 165129 is viewed about to depart from the new platform while operating 2T47, the 20.20 Cheltenham Spa to Bristol Temple Meads service, on 10 October 2018.

GWR Class 800/3 No. 800305 is seen at Bristol Temple Meads prior to operating 1A22, the 14.53 to London Paddington, on 14 October 2018. The former Royal Mail sorting office was finally demolished in April 2019 after lying empty for many years. The site is set to become a new university building.

CrossCountry Class 220 Voyager No. 220034 is seen at Bath Spa on 14 October 2018 with 1S53, the 13.23 Exeter St Davids to Edinburgh service that should have started from Plymouth but was unable to because of track damage near Teignmouth. XC services were running via Bath and Kemble due to engineering work on Filton Bank in Bristol.

After a lengthy wait, CrossCountry finally launched their first HST set with a power door conversion on 15 October 2018. Here, Class 43 power car No. 43304 leads the set's inaugural passenger run in its modified state at Tiverton Parkway operating 1V50, the 06.06 Edinburgh to Plymouth service.

A closer view of CrossCountry's modified Mark 3 HST coaches fitted with sliding doors by Wabtec at Doncaster Works. They also had toilet waste-retention tanks fitted during this refurbishment.

Mendip Rail Class 59s Nos 59005 *Kenneth J. Painter* and 59103 *Village of Mells* are seen at Westbury with 7C77, the 12.40 Acton to Merehead Quarry empty aggregates working, on 15 October 2018. These locomotives were purchased by Freightliner after they won the Mendip stone haulage contract from DB Cargo in 2019.

A pair of GWR Class 802 IETs – Nos 802018 and 802017 – are captured rounding the curve towards Dawlish Warren with 1A85, the 13.31 Newton Abbot to London Paddington service, on 20 January 2019. The 802s are fitted with uprated engines and larger fuel tanks more suited to the arduous work over the gradients in the South West.

GWR Class 800/3 No. 800314 is seen passing under a rather threatening sky on the Dawlish Sea Wall while operating 1C80, the 11.30 London Paddington to Paignton service, on 20 January 2019.

When the GWR brand was launched, it seemed unlikely that the Class 143s would be repainted, but the cascade delays meant all units eventually received the green livery. Here Nos 143617 and 143609 are standing at Exeter Central with 2F08, the 11.49 Paignton to Exmouth service, on 3 February 2019.

The carriage washer at Plymouth Laira maintenance depot is rarely pictured, despite being an essential piece of equipment. Here, GWR Class 802 No. 802015 is in the process of having its bodywork cleaned on 3 February 2019.

GWR Class 800s IETs Nos 800029 and 800015 are pictured arriving at Taunton with 1C54, the 14.03 service from London Paddington, on 27 February 2019. The angle of the light shows off the vinyl bodysides of the 800s – those on the Class 802s are painted and therefore have a shine rather than the matte effect seen here.

GWR Class 800/3 No. 800310 is seen passing St James' Park with 1C82, the 13.03 Paddington to Penzance service, on 8 February 2019, during a period of GWR services being diverted via Yeovil for three weeks due to engineering work in Whiteball Tunnel. This service was diagrammed as an HST, with the IET filling in at short notice.

A rather tatty GWR Class 153 No. 153333 pauses at Newcourt while operating 2T20, the 14.25 Exmouth to Paignton service, on 23 March 2019. This unit subsequently left GWR for a new life with Transport for Wales, hence the partially stripped paintwork. Newcourt station was opened on 4 June 2015.

In a surprising move during early 2019, GBRf took two Class 50 Alliance-owned locomotives on hire. These were duly repainted. Nos 50007 *Hercules* and 50049 *Defiance* are standing at Exeter St Davids while operating 1Z53, the 15.30 Penzance to London Waterloo return leg of 'The 50 Terminator – Phoenixed' railtour, on 23 March 2019.

Hanson-liveried Class 59/1s Nos 59101 *Village of Whatley* and 59104 *Village of Great Elm* are seen passing Cullompton with 6C28, the 11.41 Exeter Riverside Yard to Whatley Quarry empty stone working, on Saturday 6 April 2019. The operation of this working has since passed from DBC to Freightliner, but had not been running as regularly since the transfer.

A CrossCountry HST led by Class 43 power car No. 43321 is standing at Taunton while leading 1S51, the 12.25 Plymouth to Glasgow Central service, on 6 April 2019. The development of a multistorey car park and a new ticket office is ongoing at this station.

The first visit of a Class 88 locomotive to Devon and Cornwall was on 13 April 2019 when Direct Rail Services No. 88003 *Genesis* operated the 'The Springtime Cornishman' Pathfinder Tours charter with Class 68 No. 68034. Here the pair are seen at Plymouth after an unplanned fuel stop at Laira depot during the return leg.

The 1980s-built Class 150/2s have been enduring workhorses in the South West region, and with no replacement on the horizon it appears that they will continue to be for many years to come. No. 150247 is seen at Exeter St Thomas with 2T19, the 14.30 Exeter St Davids to Paignton service, on 27 April 2019.

GWR Class 802 No. 802020 is viewed at Starcross while operating 1Z91, the 14.00 Penzance to London Paddington service, on 4 May 2019. The final scheduled GWR HST working to Paignton ran later this day.

CrossCountry Class 220 Voyager No. 220009 passes Cockwood with 1E67, the 16.25 Plymouth to Leeds service, on 4 May 2019. The future of the XC franchise is currently uncertain, with the last bidding competition cancelled and Arriva's tenure extended to at least October 2023. It will be most interesting to see what happens next.

Just over the border from Devon into Cornwall, a GWR Castle HST set is seen arriving at Saltash station led by No. 43186 while operating 2C51, the 17.55 Plymouth to Penzance service, on 14 May 2019.

On 14 May 2019 Rail Operations Group Class 47 No. 47815 *Lost Boys 68–88* passes Langham Levels, Ivybridge, running around two hours early with 5V84, the 09.25 Ely Papworth Sidings to Laira depot, with barrier vehicles in tow ready to collect off-lease GWR HST vehicles the following day.

GWR Class 143 Pacer No. 143621 is seen at Taunton unusually operating 2U12, the 09.25 St James' Park to Cardiff Central service, on 16 May 2019. The sight of Pacers in service north of Taunton was infrequent in the GWR era.

GWR Class 43 HST power car No. 43093 *Old Oak Common HST Depot 1976–2018* stands at London Paddington after operating 1A79, the 06.47 service from Penzance, on 16 May 2019. This was the final week of full-length HST operation by GWR.

The body-side detail and nameplate on the special 'Legends of the Great Western' GWR HST power car No. 43093. This power car is now part of GWR's Castle fleet.

The sight, and indeed sound, of slam doors on Mark 3 coaches were once synonymous with London Paddington station, but are now confined to the 'Night Riviera' sleeper service, which still operates without power doors. This view was taken on 16 May 2019.

The HST coaches are often overlooked in favour of the power cars, but they are a huge part of the continued success of the InterCity 125, which was originally only conceived as a stopgap until the troubled Advanced Passenger Train was ready for service. The vehicle here is Trailer Standard (TS) No. 42068.

InterCity heritage-liveried Class 43 HST power car No. 43185 *Great Western* is seen at Bristol Temple Meads before operating 1A24, the 16.00 to London Paddington, on 18 May 2019. This was the final HST service on this route in normal public operation.

At first glance this looks like a normal view of London Paddington, but the mass of people at the end of the platforms betrays the fact that these four HST sets are lined up prior to their final departures from the terminus on 18 May 2019.

GWR Class 802 No. 802110 pauses at Exeter St Davids with 1A94, the 15.52 Penzance to London Paddington, on 1 June 2019. Paddington-bound trains usually stop on Platform 5 here, but this service was unable to due to it being occupied by the 2+4 HST set bound for Bristol.

DB Cargo Class 67s Nos 67024/67021 are seen passing Teignmouth with 1Z83, the 12.05 Truro to London Victoria working of the Belmond British Pullman, on 1 June 2019. This luxuriously appointed train usually visits the West Country for a weekend every year.

West Somerset Railway resident Hymek D7018 is seen arriving at Washford with the 12.03 Minehead to Bishops Lydeard service during the WSR's 2019 diesel gala on 22 June 2019. This gala marked D7018's welcome return to service after a major failure in 1995 and a subsequent lengthy rebuild.

West Country Class No. 34046 *Braunton* is a frequent performer on Saphos Trains' English Riviera Express excursions. Here, the loco is passing the Exeter Flood Relief Channel running as 1Z28, the 16:50 Kingswear to Bristol Temple Meads return leg of the tour, on 30 June 2019.

GWR Class 802/1 IET No. 802114 is pictured shortly after passing Teignmouth station with 1A87, the 12.00 Penzance to London Paddington service, on 13 July 2019.

Another GWR Class 802/1, No. 802110, is seen passing the South Devon Railway's Totnes Riverside station while operating 1A94, the 15.52 Penzance to London Paddington service, on 20 July 2019.

A view from Southern Region territory as GWR Class 158 No. 158952 stands at Salisbury with 1F16, the 11.08 Portsmouth Harbour to Cardiff Central service, on 21 July 2019. Many services on this route are now operated by Turbo units.

GWR operated four-coach HST formations using classic slam-door Mark 3s while waiting for modified sets to be released from Doncaster Works. Here No. 43162 *Exeter Panel Signal Box – 21st Anniversary 2009* is seen at Newport leading 2U18, the 13.08 Taunton to Cardiff Central service, on 15 August 2019.

CrossCountry hired two LNER HSTs on 24 August 2019 to provide additional capacity for the summer bank holiday weekend. Here one of the sets is standing at Plymouth after operating 1V46, the 06.45 service from York. Power car No. 43257 is closest to the camera, with No. 43251 out of sight at the rear.

Now to the other LNER HST hired in by XC on 24 August 2019. No. 43290 leads 1V50, the 06.06 Edinburgh to Plymouth service out of Newton Abbot, which was running just under an hour late at this point after being delayed by signalling issues, and earlier suffering a technical problem with one of the coaches. No. 43367 was the rear power car.

From January 2020 the GWR Class 143 fleet could only run coupled to a Class 150/2, due to their lack of compliance with accessibility regulations, ending the familiar sight of pairs of 143s operating the 'Devon Metro' services. Here, Nos 143603 and 143619 are seen at Exmouth with 2B82, the 17.25 to Barnstaple, on 26 August 2019.

A new depot costing £40 million has been constructed at Exeter St Davids for maintenance of the regional DMU fleet. The building also features improved train crew facilities. The facility is starting to take shape in this view taken on 6 August 2019.

GWR Class 802 No. 802113 is seen passing Totnes with 1C77, the 10.03 London Paddington to Penzance service, on 14 September 2019. The new station footbridge here was constructed during 2018, although the old bridge was not removed until March 2019.

DB Cargo Class 66 No. 66102 is seen passing Totnes with 6C12, the 10.57 Burngullow to Exeter Riverside loaded aggregates working, on 14 September 2019. This flow began in late 2018, and at one stage was running on an almost daily basis, with the wagons eventually continuing to Bow, in East London.

GWR Castle short set power car No. 43194 is pictured at Exeter St Davids on 14 September 2019 after operating 1Z58, the 19.45 special service from Okehampton, having worked from Weymouth on a charter for Okerail (the Okehampton line campaign group).

Earlier that day No. 43194 had been named *Okehampton Castle* and became the first of the twenty-three modified GWR HST short set power cars expected to carry these rather impressive nameplates, all dedicated to a castle near the routes operated by the sets.

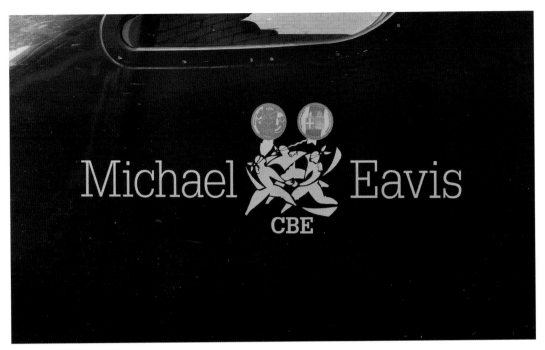

Nameplates on the IETs are of the stick-on transfer variety, carried under the cab window. This one, *Michael Eavis CBE*, is applied to No. 802013. Glastonbury Festival founder Mr Eavis also had Class 43 No. 43026 named after him.

After a long time away, GWR Class 158s are again a familiar sight on the Cornish Main Line. In this view, No. 158954 is seen at Par with 2C47, the 12.15 Exeter St Davids to Penzance service, on 21 September 2019.

BR Railfreight grey-liveried Class 26 No. 26007 became the first of the class to operate in Cornwall when it appeared at the Bodmin & Wenford Railway's 2019 diesel gala. Here, the loco arrives at Bodmin Parkway with the 15.50 arrival from Bodmin General on 15 September 2019.

GWR Class 802 No. 802102 is viewed arriving at Liskeard with 1C81, the 12.03 London Paddington to Penzance service, on a rather grey and dismal 5 October 2019.

GWR Class 802s Nos 802010 and 802008 are seen passing the overbridge at Clapperbrook Lane, Exeter, while operating 1C81, the 12.01 London Paddington to Penzance service, on 6 October 2019. This location is close to the proposed site of a new station to serve Marsh Barton Industrial Estate.

GWR Class 802/1 IET No. 802102 is seen passing Cockwood Harbour with 1A95, the 16.13 Penzance to Paddington service, on 6 October 2019. The railings beside the track were installed here in 2007, much to the annoyance of many railway photographers.

Another view from Cockwood Harbour on the same day as GWR Class 802 IETs No. 802019 and No. 802018 pass in some lovely autumn sunshine with 1C86, the 15.01 London Paddington to Penzance service.

A GWR Castle set led by No. 43040 is viewed passing Stapleton Road with 2E44, the 16.41 Bristol Temple Meads to Worcester Shrub Hill service, on 13 October 2019. This was a short-lived HST diagram. The pair of tracks on the left were completed in December 2018 after a three-year construction period, giving vital extra capacity between Filton Abbey Wood and Temple Meads.

GWR Class 802 IETs Nos 802020 and 802016 are seen on the Dawlish Sea Wall with 1A85, the 11.01 Penzance to London Paddington service, on 27 October 2019. Despite being specified as 'Dawlish-proof', there have been incidents of the new trains suffering technical issues, such as engines shutting down, after being hit by waves on this exposed section of line.

On-track plant is an important but often overlooked part of maintaining a twenty-first-century railway. Here Colas Rail-operated Plasser & Theurer tamping machine No. DR73920 is seen on the Dawlish Sea Wall with 6J81, the 09.27 Castle Cary to Crediton (via Plymouth) working, on 27 October 2019. This was the part of the sea wall rebuilt after the 2014 storm.

GWR have reformed a number of their three-carriage Class 158/9s into two-car sets. Nos 158767 and 158750 are two such units, and are pictured at Filton Abbey Wood with 1F23, the 14.30 Cardiff Central to Portsmouth, on 11 November 2019 – though the service was curtailed at Fratton due to a track circuit failure.

Rail Operations Group Class 37 No. 37884 *Cepheus* is seen passing Newport running as 5Q78, the 10.52 Hornsey depot to Newport Docks, hauling former Great Northern Class 313 EMUs No. 313061 and No. 313039 for scrap on 11 November 2019. The electrification went live in South Wales over Christmas of that year.

GWR Class 802 IET No. 802002 is captured standing at Castle Cary with 1A87, the 14.45 service to London Paddington, on 12 November 2019. The line to and from Taunton was closed for engineering work.

GWR Class 43 No. 43156 *Dartington International Summer School* is seen at Bristol Temple Meads trailing a classic 2+4 short HST set with 2U22, the 15.44 Weston-super-Mare to Cardiff Central service, on 12 November 2019.

GWR Class 800/3 No. 800311 ascending the incline towards Exeter Central while operating 1A90, the 13.51 Plymouth to London Paddington service, on 14 November 2019. This was the penultimate day of GWR services being diverted via Honiton and Yeovil for six days due to engineering work taking place in the Taunton area.

A view of GWR Class 165 No. 165131 arriving at Gloucester with 2G83, the 12.15 Swindon to Cheltenham Spa service, on 16 November 2019.

The new footbridge at Totnes station provides a good vantage point, though not one suited to shorter photographers due to the high sides. In this image, GWR Class 802 IET No. 802014 is seen arriving with 1A83, the 09.45 Penzance to London Paddington service, on 17 November 2019.

Since first running during the 2018 festive season, the 'Train of Lights' has been a hugely successful venture for the Paignton & Dartmouth Steam Railway. It features over 1,000 lights, both on the train and on the side of the track. In this image, the 18.45 service to Kingswear stands at the Paignton Queen's Park terminus trailed by No. 75014 *Braveheart* on 1 December 2019.

Since the December 2019 timetable change, Class 158s are now the usual offering on the 'Tarka Line', with services having a more even frequency, but now terminating at St James' Park instead of Exmouth. Here, No. 158957 arrives at Crediton with 2J87, the 13.35 Barnstaple to St James' Park, on 22 January 2020.

Passengers at London Paddington are boarding First GWR Class 800/3 IET No. 800306 as it waits to operate 1B11, the 10.47 service to Swansea, on 25 January 2020.

TfL Rail took over stopping services between Paddington and Heathrow Airport/Reading ahead of the full Crossrail operation through Central London scheduled to finally start by summer 2022. Class 345 Aventura No. 345008 is seen at Hayes and Harlington after operating 9T49, the 10.48 service from London Paddington, on 25 January 2020.

Construction in progress at West Ealing with a new ticket office and footbridge being built to replace the rather cramped previous offerings. TfL Class 345 No. 345008 passes under the structure of the new bridge while operating 9T65, the 12.48 Paddington to Hayes service, on 25 January 2020.

Services on the Greenford branch line are still operated by GWR, but now terminate at West Ealing instead of Paddington. Here, Class 165 No. 165133 stands at Greenford station, which is shared with the London Underground Central Line, on 25 January 2020.

Services on the Cornish Main Line from Plymouth to Penzance were upgraded to a half-hourly frequency in the December 2019 timetable change. In this view, GWR Class 800/3 No. 800319 is at the end of the line after operating 1C76, the 10.02 Paddington to Penzance service, on 1 February 2020.

Network Rail's Class 950 unit No. 950001 is a frequent visitor to the Great Western network. This unique purpose-built track recording unit is based on a Class 150/1 bodyshell. Here, the distinctive Sprinter is seen at Bristol Temple Meads after operating a lengthy testing circuit from Exeter on 8 February 2020.

A GWR Castle HST set led by Class 43 No. 43016 is pictured arriving at a fully electrified Patchway with 2C77, the 13.00 Cardiff Central to Penzance service, on 8 February 2020.

GWR Class 166 No. 166203 is seen at Bristol Temple Meads while operating 2C30, the 18.42 Gloucester to Frome service, on 8 February 2020. First Great Western blue was still very much alive and kicking into the new decade!

Regardless of how many other changes are on the way, we end with what is expected to be a very common sight for many years to come – a GWR IET taking another load of passengers to the capital. This is Class 802 No. 802111 passing Cullompton with 1A86, the 13.13 Plymouth to London Paddington, on 12 February 2020.